BASIC
TENNIS
ILLUSTRATED

BASIC TENNIS ILLUSTRATED

Merritt Cutler

Dover Publications, Inc., New York

Published in Canada by General Publishing Company, Ltd., 30 Lesmill Road, Don Mills, Toronto, Ontario M3B 2T6.
Published in the United Kingdom by Constable and Company, Ltd., 10 Orange Street, London WC2H 7EG.

This Dover edition, first published in 1980, is an unabridged republication of the work originally published by the McGraw-Hill Book Company in 1967 under the title *The Tennis Book*.

International Standard Book Number: 0-486-24006-1
Library of Congress Catalog Card Number: 80-65738

Manufactured in the United States of America
Dover Publications, Inc.
180 Varick Street
New York, N.Y. 10014

To William T. Tilden II

I would like to express my appreciation
to Mrs. Gladys Heldman, editor of *World Tennis,*
for her encouragement and help.

Preface

It was in 1908 and I was ten years old when I began playing tennis. The most unusual fact about all of this was that my family had very moderate means, and at that time tennis was a game for rich men and their families, or at least the well-to-do. Tennis was also considered by most of my friends to be a sissy game.

It did happen, though, that while there were very few clubs at that time, particularly in my town, I grew up near one. When I was fourteen I won the men's championship, and the club considered me a comer. Their pride in me was such that they dug into the club treasury to send me to Forest Hills to take lessons. The members wanted me to have the advantages of which they had been deprived. I have always been very grateful.

This was in 1913. The pro at Forest Hills was George Agutter, a former Wimbledon ball boy and famous teacher. He taught the Continental grip, and I had been using the Western grip. Eventually I came around to the Eastern grip, which was just beginning to be used, and is the generally accepted grip today.

My days as a junior member of the West Side Tennis Club were very exciting, and I had the pleasure of watching players like Norris Williams, Maurice McGloughlin, Billy Johnston and the Australians, Norman Brookes and Anthony Wilding, while they were here for Davis Cup matches.

However, my big passion outside of tennis was drawing and painting. As my involvement in drawing seemed to retard me in my other high school subjects, my father (a frustrated artist) decided to withdraw me and go all out for art. He enrolled me in Pratt Institute in Brooklyn.

When the First World War broke out, I enlisted in the 7th Regiment National Guard, which became the 107th U.S. Infantry. After several months' training we embarked for France. Upon arrival, our division, the 27th, was assigned as a gesture of Allied friendship to the Second British Army under Sir Douglas Haig. My interest in drawing persisted and I made myself a canvas container for a sketchbook to be slung over my shoulder. I intended to return home with an artist's impression of the war, one that would make me famous. My sketchbook was taken from me later at a review by General Pershing. It was considered to be improper equipment.

While we were in the trenches near Mount Kemmel in Belgium, my friend Percy Hall, a lieutenant in my company, told me that he had seen at headquarters a bulletin announcing a tennis tournament to be held at Cannes for eligible A.E.F. personnel. It sounded awfully good to me, particularly at that time, so I put in a request to go. I must have been considered more valuable where I was, for I heard no more of it. This was a decision that was almost fatal to me. Percy was later killed at the Hindenburg Line.

When I returned home I found it necessary to support myself and obtained a job in the art department of a large advertising agency. My interest in tennis had not waned, but I found it difficult, with my full-time work, to play in any of the large tournaments, only a few of which were in or near New York. I remember being beaten on grass at the old Crescent Athletic Club in the Eastern Grass Court Tournament by Ellsworth Vines, a newcomer from the West. He won the National Championship that year.

In the winter, things were more evened up for me because I could play on the indoor courts of my old regiment, the 7th (the National Indoor Championship was held there), and I could practice quite a bit, after work and weekends.

With my partner Perrine Rockefellow, I was fortunate enough to win the National Indoor Doubles Championship in 1930.

I began years ago to analyze the strokes by making sketches of various phases of their execution, and also because I admired the wonderful movements the body is capable of. So this book has two purposes: one is to show how the strokes are made; the other is to show and dramatize what I feel is the beauty of the human body as it plays this game. Thus the text has been kept to a minimum.

Seeing how a thing is done seems to me to be the best way of learning anything involving movement. The best way to learn tennis is to take some lessons at the outset from a competent pro. Eight years old is not too young to start. But for both young and old, the pro's great value lies in watching and correcting mistakes which, if allowed to become confirmed habit, hamper the player's progress later.

This does not mean that the professional will insist on an exact grip or restrict movements to an exact manner. He will simply keep the player from doing things he knows from experience retard smoothness of execution.

Style in playing tennis is something that will develop gradually and differently in each individual, so no particular player's style should be copied, no matter how effective that player is.

Incidentally, it is surprising to see how much the styles of the great players differ. (By style, I mean obvious mannerisms which are often misleading.) Underneath these mannerisms, they all have the important basic qualities in common: for example, smoothness of execution based on a sound knowledge of stroke production, a perfect sense of timing, fine condition and body control and other important values. If you add *intelligence* to all of these qualities, you have a real player.

So try to get the underlying feel of each stroke, rather than fussing about the details of whether each finger is in place, and so on. In fact, there are strokes in this book that should not be attempted by beginners, such as the spin shots. Concentrate on the basic forehand and backhand drives until you can make them smoothly and consistently, and then work on the volley and continue from there.

The good, steady club player, however, may improve his game by adding variety, particularly spin, for many a seasoned player has had the rhythm of his game broken by change of pace, depth and spin by a less steady opponent.

Many of the great players have written books about how they played the game. My drawings and text are based on a study of the stroke production of many great players, from Tilden to the present. I have tried to show a composite of their execution, the things they have in common, leaving out the personal mannerisms; thus none of the drawings is of a particular player except where a player is named.

There are so many facets to tennis that I feel the game cannot be completely covered in one book. Therefore I have confined myself to what I consider the essentials of stroke production and simple tactics.

Contents

BASIC
TENNIS
ILLUSTRATED

The Forehand Grip

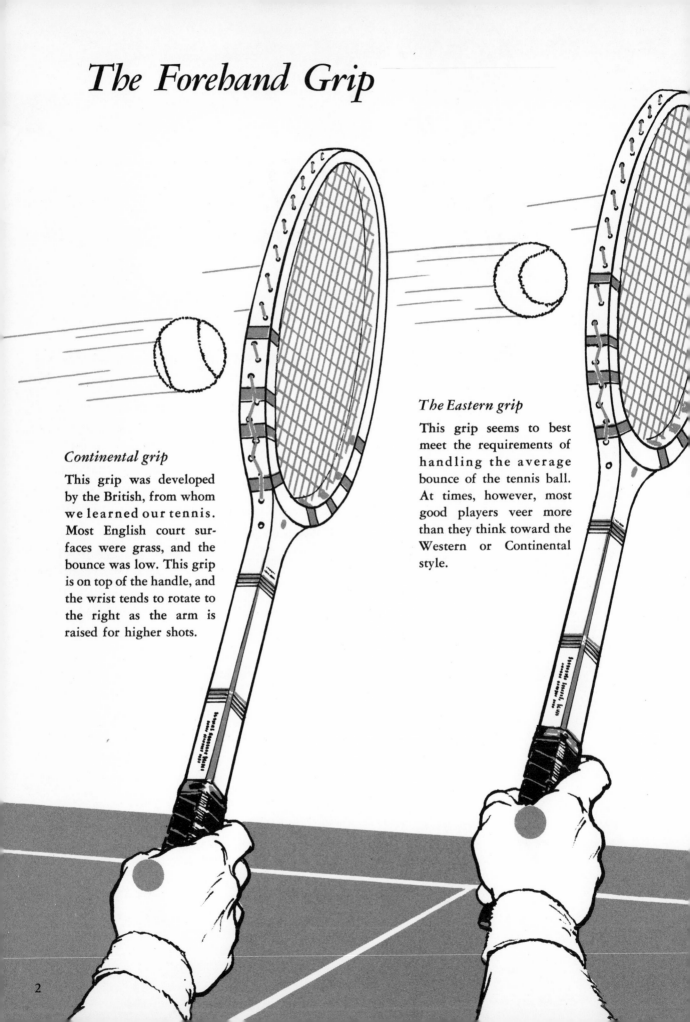

Continental grip

This grip was developed by the British, from whom we learned our tennis. Most English court surfaces were grass, and the bounce was low. This grip is on top of the handle, and the wrist tends to rotate to the right as the arm is raised for higher shots.

The Eastern grip

This grip seems to best meet the requirements of handling the average bounce of the tennis ball. At times, however, most good players veer more than they think toward the Western or Continental style.

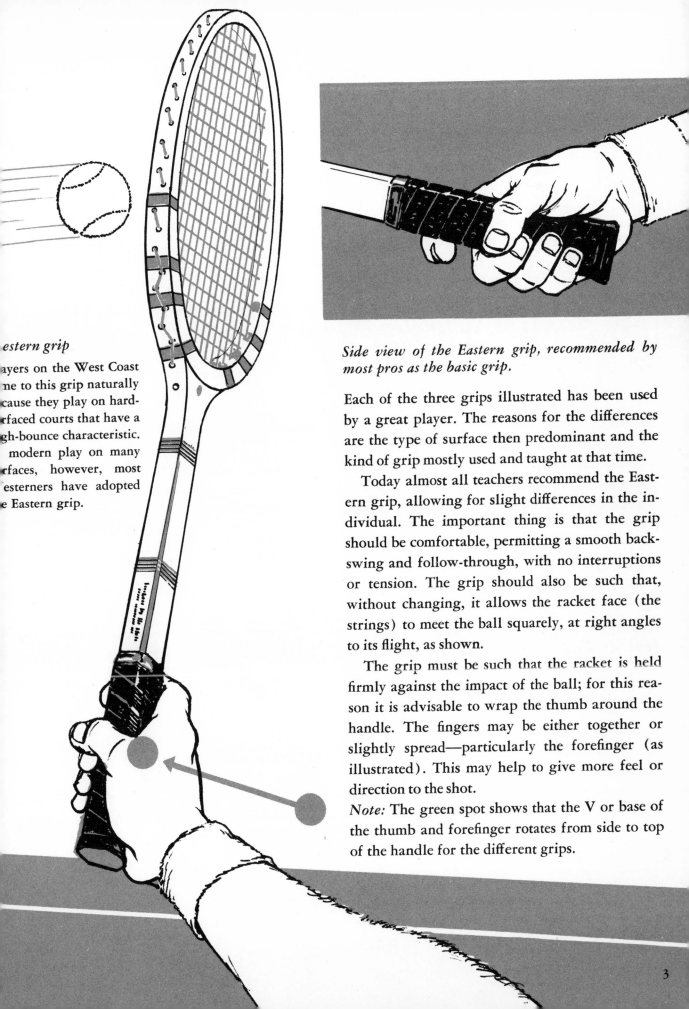

estern grip

...ayers on the West Coast
...ne to this grip naturally
...cause they play on hard-
...rfaced courts that have a
...gh-bounce characteristic.

...modern play on many
...rfaces, however, most
...esterners have adopted
...e Eastern grip.

Side view of the Eastern grip, recommended by most pros as the basic grip.

Each of the three grips illustrated has been used by a great player. The reasons for the differences are the type of surface then predominant and the kind of grip mostly used and taught at that time.

Today almost all teachers recommend the Eastern grip, allowing for slight differences in the individual. The important thing is that the grip should be comfortable, permitting a smooth backswing and follow-through, with no interruptions or tension. The grip should also be such that, without changing, it allows the racket face (the strings) to meet the ball squarely, at right angles to its flight, as shown.

The grip must be such that the racket is held firmly against the impact of the ball; for this reason it is advisable to wrap the thumb around the handle. The fingers may be either together or slightly spread—particularly the forefinger (as illustrated). This may help to give more feel or direction to the shot.

Note: The green spot shows that the V or base of the thumb and forefinger rotates from side to top of the handle for the different grips.

3

The Forehand Drive

Backswing

The forehand drive is the most frequently used and therefore the most important stroke in tennis. A sound, well-produced forehand leads to a good game.

Let us take a look here at a good forehand drive, executed by a right-handed player from a stationary position (as when receiving service). The player faces his opponent with feet comfortably separated to give a solid stance, and with knees slightly bent. He leans forward a little, the racket held easily across the body and cradled lightly at its throat by the fingers of the left hand. As the ball leaves the opponent's racket its line of flight must be judged quickly (in this case to the receiver's right). The left foot moves forward and to the right; at the same time the body turns until the left shoulder is pointing toward the net. Simultaneously the swing of the racket toward the back has begun, with the racket head leading across the body on about the level of the eyes, continuing to a com-

fortable extension of the arm (elbow and wri slightly bent) down and forward in a smoot elliptical movement (see diagram).

Immediately after the racket head has started i forward swing, the player's body starts its forwar thrust from the right foot and continues a forwar movement along with the swing in order to impa power.

The ball should be contacted at a point opposi the left foot. The racket face (the strings) mee the ball squarely in a somewhat upward direction At no point may this forward upward swing of th racket stop or even hesitate. It should continu even after the ball is met, as though the ball wer not there, the arm fully extended. The ball shoul actually be carried on the racket about two feet t give control and power. As the ball leaves th racket, the slight upward swing and the natura turnover of the wrist at this point impart topspi to the ball and help control its line of flight.

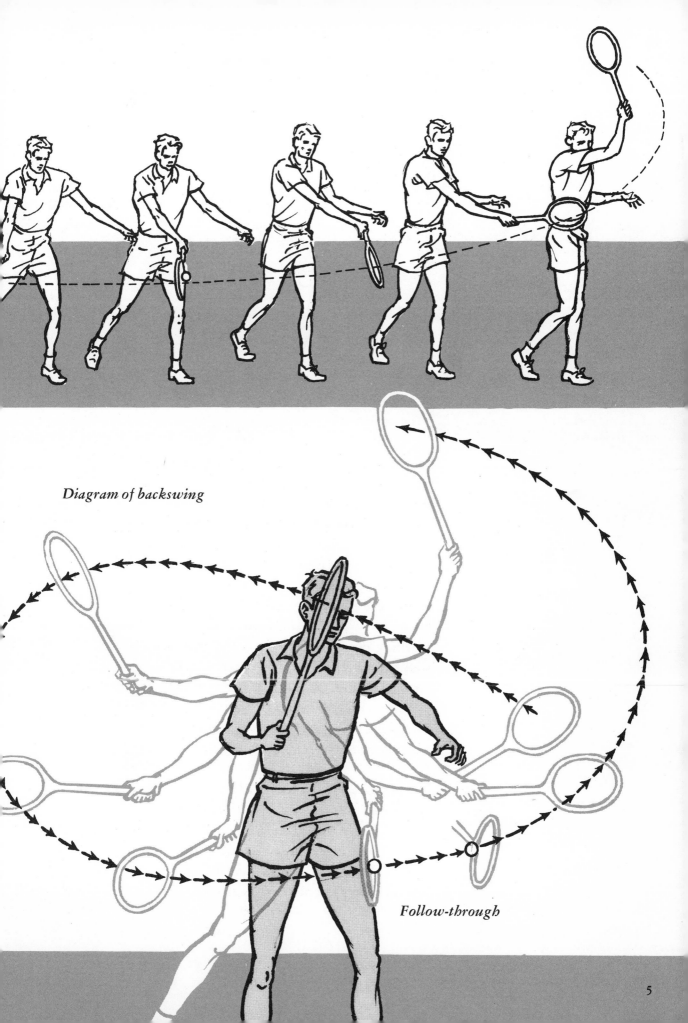

Diagram of backswing

Follow-through

The Running Forehand Drive

Follow-through

The forehand drive executed while running (which will be most of the time) is much the same shot as the stationary one. The backswing, which must still be fluid, will frequently be shorter because of both the necessity of maintaining balance and lack of time. Balance is of the greatest importance, and good timing is essential. The stride must be gauged so that the player arrives at the hitting area with his left foot coming forward as the racket does, touching down as the ball is hit, with the body well balanced. Of course the body will be moving into the shot; if the shot is properly hit this factor often gives the most power with the least effort. The swing and the pivoting of shoulders, particularly the follow-through, are as described on page 4.

Pictured at the right is William T. Tilden, who epitomized all the qualities of a great player—grace, balance, timing and fluidity. Unfortunately, these tennis virtues cannot be taught, but constant practice under good supervision will bring out the best the individual player possesses.

The Backhand Grip

The backhand grip must be comfortable and allow for an uninterrupted fluid backswing and follow-through. It must also allow the racket face to meet the ball squarely through the hitting zone without adjustment of position. The backhand grip most players use approximates the opposite of the Eastern forehand grip—with the wrist about the same extent behind the handle on the opposite side so as to give a hit and not a pull.

Most good players place the thumb *along* the handle, where it acts as a brace against the ball's impact. The hammer grip, with the thumb *around* the handle, is all right if you are able to hold the racket firmly enough.

The Hammer grip

The Orthodox grip

The Backhand Drive

The forehand and backhand drives are described here as the basic strokes in returning the normal waist-high shot. Depending on the player's position in the court, they can be either defensive or offensive. *Drive* means a ball met with good balance and hit fairly flat. Spin shots will be taken up later.

Although the backhand drive is hit with a different grip, the backswing, the balance, the turn of the body, and the follow-through should be a replica in reverse of the forehand drive.

(*Right:* the poise and smooth swing of Ellsworth Vines's great backhand shot)

The Running Backhand Drive

In executing a backhand drive while running, if possible for body balance shorten the steps as you approach the ball, and try to have the weight on the right foot as the ball is hit. The backswing should be shorter than in a stationary shot. If the ball has to be hit low, get down to it by bending the knees. Sometimes you will be really stretched all out to reach the ball (right). In this case take the racket head back with the wrist, hit with wrist and short arm movement, and follow through.

The Left-handed Player

Backswing

The same principles and moves involved in stroke production from the right apply in reverse for the left-hander.

The left-handed player, however, must guard against a few tendencies: for instance, as he hits cross-court to the right-hander's backhand he is likely to develop a very "whippy" or wristy shot that can become too loose or sloppy. On his backhand to the right-hander's backhand he must hit straight down the line, and to play it safely he too often reverts to a sliced or cramped shot. This can be corrected by moving the left shoulder farther around and down to the ball. Topspin will add further control to the shot.

The left-hander's advantage is mostly psychological. He is used to playing right-handers, whereas the right-hander finds his opponent's backhand on the wrong side. Even cognizant of the fact, he too often by habit finds himself attacking what turns out to be a strong forehand.

Follow-through

Balance of Power

Speed of the ball in flight means how fast the ball travels.

Pace on the ball means a ball that feels heavy when it hits the racket. A ball without pace feels light on the racket and is much easier to handle; a ball with much pace on it can actually jolt the racket. A ball with great pace may travel through the air with less speed than one that feels like a feather on the racket. Nevertheless, a ball may have both speed and pace.

The ball that has pace is hit with the weight of the body behind it as well as with a smooth swing and follow-through. The player has not hit *at* the ball, but *through* it; the stroke has been started from the foot on the side where the stroke begins and up through the leg, the body moving forward with the swing.

A ball that is very fast through the air, on the other hand, may be hit with just the arm—with no body behind it. It is difficult when you are moving about the court, often barely able to reach the ball, to obtain the solid stance necessary to get the body behind a shot.

The player shown on the facing page seems to have this solidity and appears about to go all out for a winner, with good pace straight down the line. He had better make it, because this flat-footed stance is not conducive to a quick getaway.

This player has planted his right foot to take his weight and start the swing, but when he hits the ball the left foot will be more in front to take the weight shift. If he intended to go in to the net, the left foot would be more in front at this time for a quick takeoff, but possibly with some loss of power on the shot.

The Volley

The volley is an offensive shot and probably accounts for more winners than any other single stroke. There are many different kinds of volley, but the big thing to remember is that this is a shot that has to be built up to and prepared for by mastering the ground strokes. Forget the volley until you have established a foundation of sound ground strokes—forehand and backhand—strokes you can control, place with confidence, and follow in to the net.

The volley should be made from within ten feet of the net after you have made a forcing drive, which presumably has allowed you to take a commanding position.

If your opponent makes an unexpectedly fine return that you are extended to reach, you are still in the driver's seat because of your position at the net. In such a case, instead of trying a put-away the first volley, hit it to build up an easy return. (In a sense, there is no such thing as a defensive volley; if you do have to volley defensively, you have

probably used bad judgment in going to the net without a sufficiently forcing shot.)

There have been players who have been considered great volleyers because they made so many sensational volleys; actually, they should not have been forced to make such difficult shots.

One classic example took place during a match between Bill Tilden and René La Coste of France in 1926. Tilden was the great all-court player— fine ground strokes and splendid volleys. La Coste was known as the perfect, machinelike back-court player, but he was no volleyer. Tilden obviously felt he had to win from the net, yet when he came in he either was passed or forced into error.

The thing that impressed me most was the fact that La Coste, even though he came in to the net sparingly, always seemed to win the point, and it always seemed to be at a crucial point. In this instance La Coste won the match and our National Championship.

The Forehand Volley

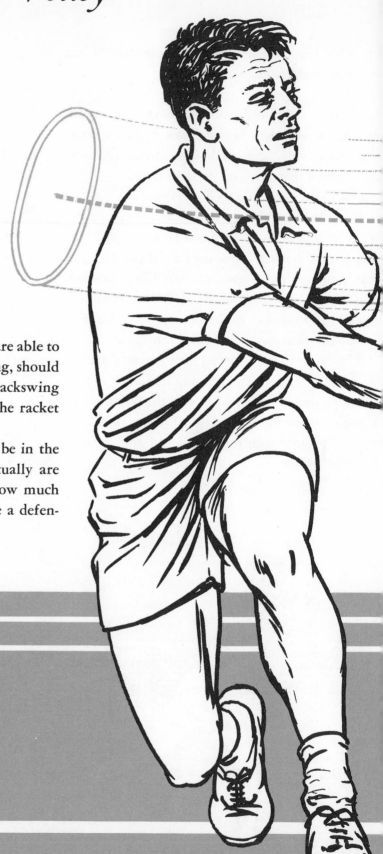

The average forehand volley which you are able to reach in good balance and with an opening, should be a precise shot hit firmly, with short backswing a little in front of the body, and with the racket tilted back slightly to give underspin.

When you are at the net you should be in the commanding position. Whether you actually are depends on your preceding shot and how much you have forced your opponent to make a defensive return.

The Backhand Volley

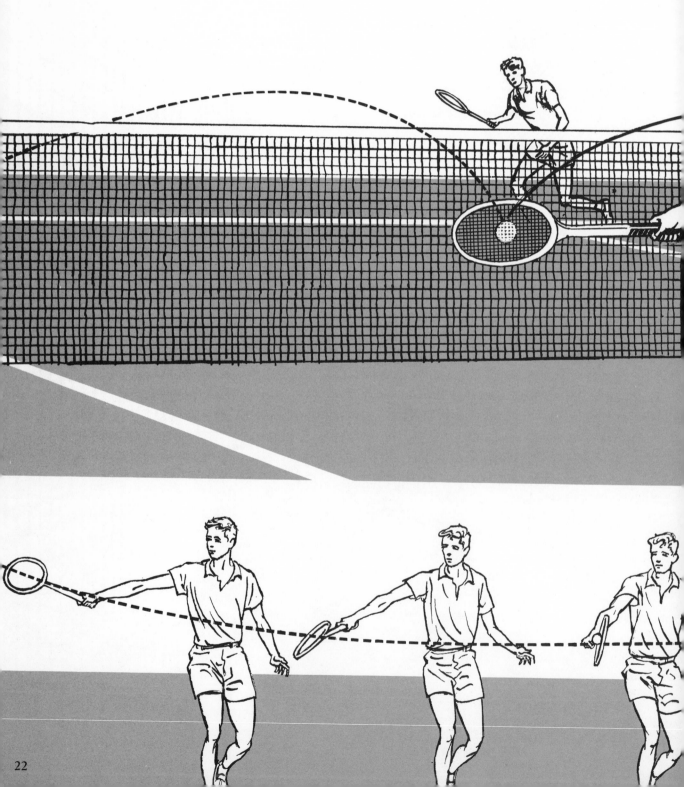

The backhand volley—hit, like the forehand volley, with a short backswing and short follow-through—is a punch shot. The racket face at contact should be tilted slightly back to give bite, backspin, and control. The forceful deep volley should be varied with the shorter sharply angled volley as the occasion requires and for surprise. You should not repeat any shot so frequently that your opponent knows what you are going to do.

The High Forehand Volley

This shot is something between an overhead and the usual volley. Hit it as a volley, with short back-swing and a firm wrist just a little in front of the body, tilting the racket face back slightly.

The Low Volley

This is a volley you will not make from choice. You are probably close to the net; if you were not you would let the ball bounce and either half-volley or hit it on the rise. The low volley is one of the most difficult tennis shots: since you are hitting from well below the top of the net, you must hit up, making it a defensive strike. Your volley must depend on touch (not hitting hard, but with feel and control) and will most likely be an angled shot with underspin.

Your opponent will realize your difficulties and know that your only chance is a soft short shot; in anticipation he will probably be coming in. Your answer to this could be an unexpected volley lob, a very difficult shot over his head. But unless you have guessed right and your lob is perfect, you have set up an easy overhead winner for him. The best shot is usually a short, soft return that will force your opponent to come in and hit from below the level of the net. Then you must be ready for the possibility that his return will be a lob. And, if your soft return is not good and bounces too high, he probably has an easy drive winner.

The Running Forehand Volley

In a running volley in which you have to reach for the ball, there is no backswing. The hit is all forward and short, meeting the ball a little in front of the body toward the net. Move the racket head into the ball, using the wrist and arm to impel it, in place of the backswing. The face of the racket is tilted slightly back to give bite.

Pictured here is Althea Gibson, one of the best women volleyers of recent years, making the shot.

The Forehand
Drop Volley

This shot can often be a winner where a hard-hit volley would lose the point. One factor governing the choice of this shot is the type of court being played on. A very fast court favors the flat fast volley, either deep or angled. But many times on slow courts I have seen the overzealous player at the net bang the ball, only to have it retrieved or even returned past him. The forehand drop volley is simple but requires a touch—the ability to change pace—many hard-hitting players do not have. A short swing, stopped at impact, with the racket face laid back to impart some backspin to the ball—this shot is very much like the bunt in baseball.

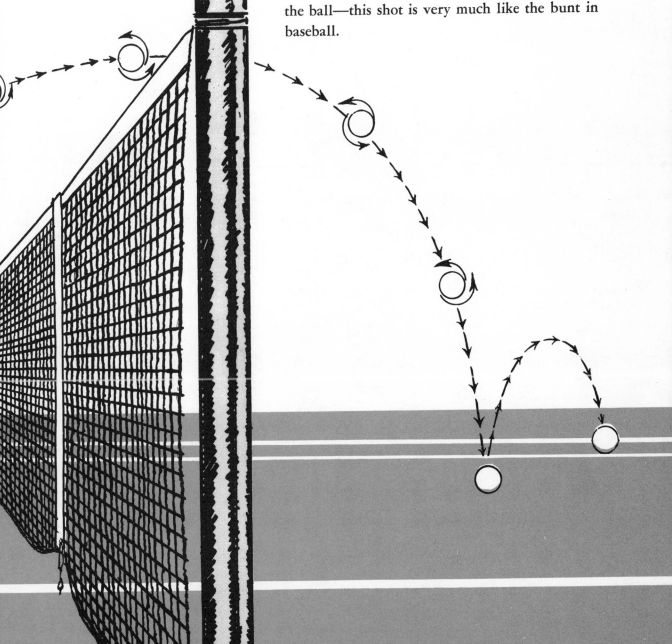

The Backhand Drop Volley

All the things said about the forehand drop volley apply to this shot as well. This should be a surprise shot, a shot for change of pace. It is also a shot that must be really well made; if it is anticipated and not short enough, you are practically giving the point away.

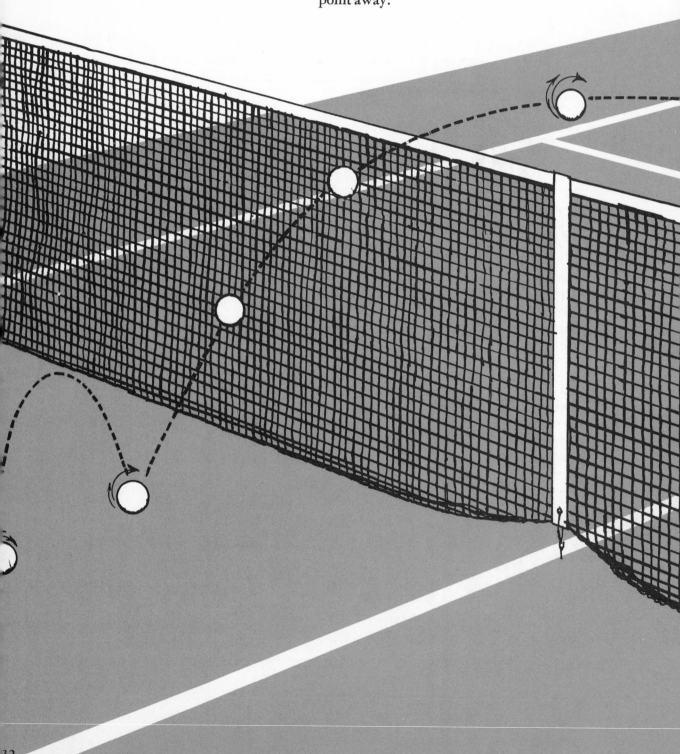

The Half-volley

While "half-volley" distinguishes the shot, the name is not quite right. The ball bounces before it is hit, but the hit is close to the ground. It is not a shot that a player chooses to play, but is almost always the result of not getting in far enough toward the net to volley the ball so it is usually made from around the service line. As the shot is low, be sure to bend the knees; and as there is not much time, take a shorter backswing than in the drive. Hit through smoothly but with less follow-through than in the drive; this shot should not be hit as hard. Keep the racket face open in order to clear the net. The rest is timing.

(*Opposite:* Maria Bueno, the great Brazilian player, making a very low half-volley. This shot may be blocked with practically no backswing and just dunked over the net like a drop shot. Notice that the racket face is very open.)

Grip for the Serve and Overhead

Most good players use the same grip to serve as they do to hit the overhead smash. With the majority it is the Continental grip shown on page 2, with edge of the racket face toward the player; others turn it a little more toward the backhand grip, page 8. The fingers will be a little more spread, particularly the forefinger, as this gives more feel and control of the racket head.

The Serve

The serve is the only shot in tennis that is completely under your control. You toss it and you hit it. It is comparable to being allowed the first punch in a prize fight, so you should win it. The average player should not consistently try to score an ace on the first serve. By good speed and placement, force a defensive return; if you miss, your second ball is your insurance. However, your second serve must not be so soft that it is a pushover. Learn to put more topspin on it to give it more margin of safety and try to outguess the receiver, as a pitcher does a batter.

There are three basic serves: the flat serve, the American twist, and the slice serve, illustrated on page 42. The swing is the same on all three, and the power comes not by a hit but by the smoothness of the swing and the forward thrust of the body behind it.

Be sure your opponent is ready. Then stand with your left foot slightly behind the baseline and your left side toward the net. The movement of tossing the ball and starting the backward swing of the racket begins simultaneously. The ball should be tossed high enough to be struck at the full extent of the arm but not so high that there is any wait for it to come down. The timing and the exact height for the racket to meet the ball without hesitation in the swing can only be achieved by practice. The racket should almost scrape the back on the first loop of the swing and then hit with the arm almost straight.

Side View of the Service Swing

Notice the relaxed stance, with the weight even balanced on both feet, legs straight but knees stiff. As the ball is tossed and the racket starts backswing, the body begins to shift its weight

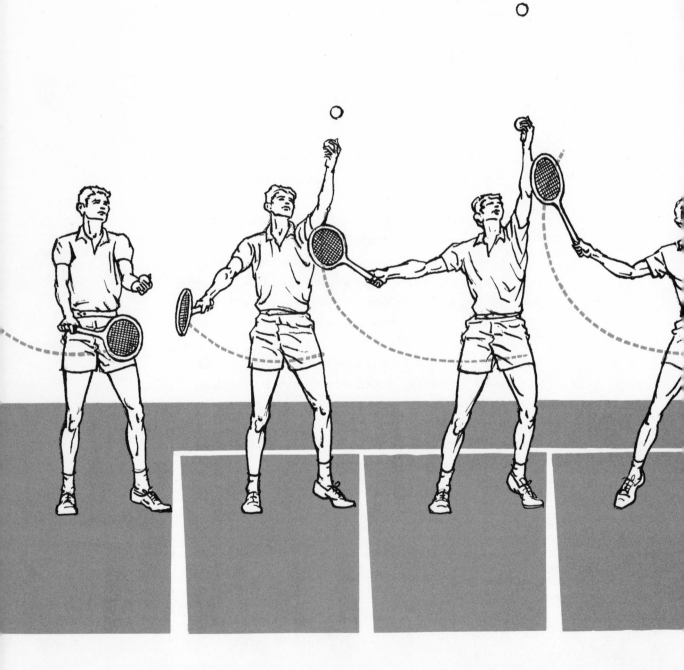

left foot and rises on it; the body bends slightly
backward with the eyes fastened on the ball. The
racket almost scrapes the back on the first loop of
the double swing and as the second loop starts upward the body is on the left toes and moving forward. The racket should meet the ball slightly in
front of the body. A common mistake is hitting it
too far in front, thereby losing power. It is a
smooth swing and fluid body motion which gives
the power, not extreme exertion or muscle.

Neither foot may touch the line or the ground
inside the line before the ball is struck.

Be sure your opponent is ready before serving.

Avoid foot faults.

Do not walk up to the line without coming to a
complete stop before serving.

The Three
Principal Serves

The Slice Serve. This is the most useful serve. swing is the same but the ball is tossed slightl the right of the head and a little forward. The ward swing will aim at the upper right side of ball, which will travel from right to left thro the air, and when it bounces will continue in same direction as a result of the right-to-left sp

e American Twist Serve. This serve is difficult
d not for the average player. The ball is tossed
ove the left shoulder. On the upward swing, the
ket head is down with the wrist cocked and
own into the ball on the lower-left side by wrist
pped up and over toward the upper right. The
l's flight is from your right to left and bounces
the opposite direction.

The Flat Serve is hit with the same swing but with
the strings facing flat toward the opposite court.
The lack of spin makes it a faster serve but harder
to control. It should only be tried by a tall man
player, and not at all by women.

Finish of slice serve.

43

Receiving the Serve

Stand in the ready position about on the baseline and where a line from you to the server will bisect your service court. Be on your toes ready to turn right or left as you see the direction of the serve. Do not take it on the rise unless it is a high bounce such as the twist serve described on page 43. If your opponent's first serve is a slice to your forehand, very often you might stand a little to the right to give you a jump on it. Don't stand left of center to favor your backhand side; this leaves you open for a slice serve (the most used) and is a giveaway that you have a weak backhand.

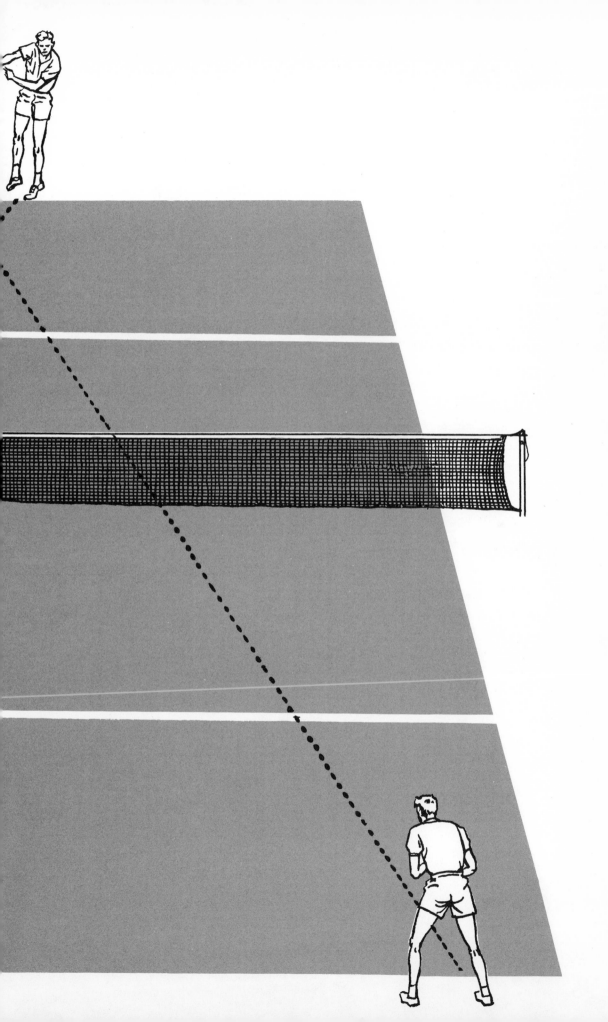

The Recovery Shot

When you have been forced to run hard to reach a ball which bounces low in the far corner of your court and close to the baseline, you are on the defensive. Chances are your opponent has come in to the net. Do not try a hard passing shot but toss up a lob, and be sure it is deep. The other alternative would be a high, slow topspin shot down the line. These two shots would give you time to recover and get back near the center of your court, whereas the return of your hard shot would leave you flat-footed. This advice holds particularly true for the ladies.

The Lob

There is no more important defensive shot than the lob, and a fine lob can be offensive. It should be practiced faithfully and is too often neglected. When your opponent has hit a very hard, well-placed drive and has taken the net, your chances of passing him are probably no better than one out of

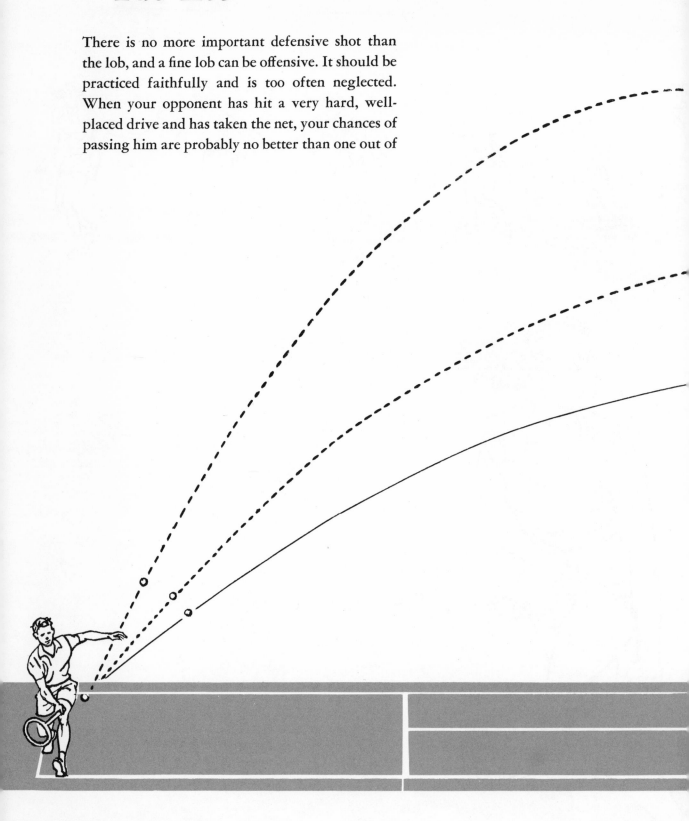

ten. A very good lob will drive him back to the baseline and many times allow you to take the net. Seldom are even the best players able to put away a lob that is within a foot or two of the baseline. This is simply a lifted shot made with usual backswing. If you can at times put topspin or underspin on the lob it probably makes it more difficult to handle. But by all means the shot's accuracy and depth are most important.

This lob is too high and too short. Let it bounce before hitting it.

Too short. This lob can be killed.

The perfect lob. Good speed, out of reach, lands close to the baseline.

The Overhead Smash

This shot of course is the answer to the lob. Assuming that you can get under the lob with your body in balance ready to hit, in most cases it should be a winning shot. It is hit like the serve except that the big swing is not taken, the racket is poised behind the back in the ready position. The left arm will point toward the ball for balance, the knees slightly flexed. As the ball is hit at the full extent of the arm, the body is moving slightly forward.

Most overheads should be hit flat and hard like the cannonball serve, the force coming from a smooth swing.

The alternate overhead shot, particularly when the opponent is far back and fast at reaching hard shots, is a soft sliced overhead to the sideline.

The Spin Shots

It seems to me that spin shots are greatly neglected today, and this is reflected in the fact that they are seldom used and are even scorned by most of our best players. If a player as great as Bill Tilden considered spin very important, I do not see how it can be ignored, although I agree that before it is considered, the basic flat ground strokes should be mastered. Spin is not for beginners, but I believe it should be part of the equipment of any player with any claim to being a serious tournament contestant. My reason for including the spin shots in this book is that they seem to have been neglected in all the books written since Tilden's *Match Play and Spin of the Ball*.

It has been said that "the best defense is a good offense," which is all right if it works; but certainly a great defense is most valuable, particularly where a long match is involved. No player can keep up an attack over a five-set match, particularly on a hot day.

I have noticed that quite a few of our best players use an underspin backhand return and call it a chip shot. The trouble is they do it too often and, one is led to believe, it is because they do not have a good orthodox backhand drive. The spin shot— whether top, side, or underspin—should be used

purposefully, and mixed with the orthodox flat drive for change. The only other purpose of a spin shot is purely defensive.

When you are stretched all out to reach a ball with no time for backswing, the shot must be almost all wrist. In this case it seems that with the racket face turned slightly back you can get more grip or control of the ball and, of course, it will have some backspin.

The purposeful uses of the spin shot are for the following reasons:

1. To take the pace off of an opponent's hard, speedy drives and slow up the tempo. To break up his rhythm.

2. Spin on a shot gives you more control. For instance, on a sharply angled cross-court drive topspin can keep the ball in the court. On the second service, topspin allows the ball to be hit hard, with more margin of safety.

3. Spin on the ball affects its bounce, higher or lower, and tends to throw off the opponent's timing. The bounce will vary on different surfaces.

4. And spin takes effect on the opponent's racket, throwing the ball upward or downward from his intended line of flight, often causing an error.

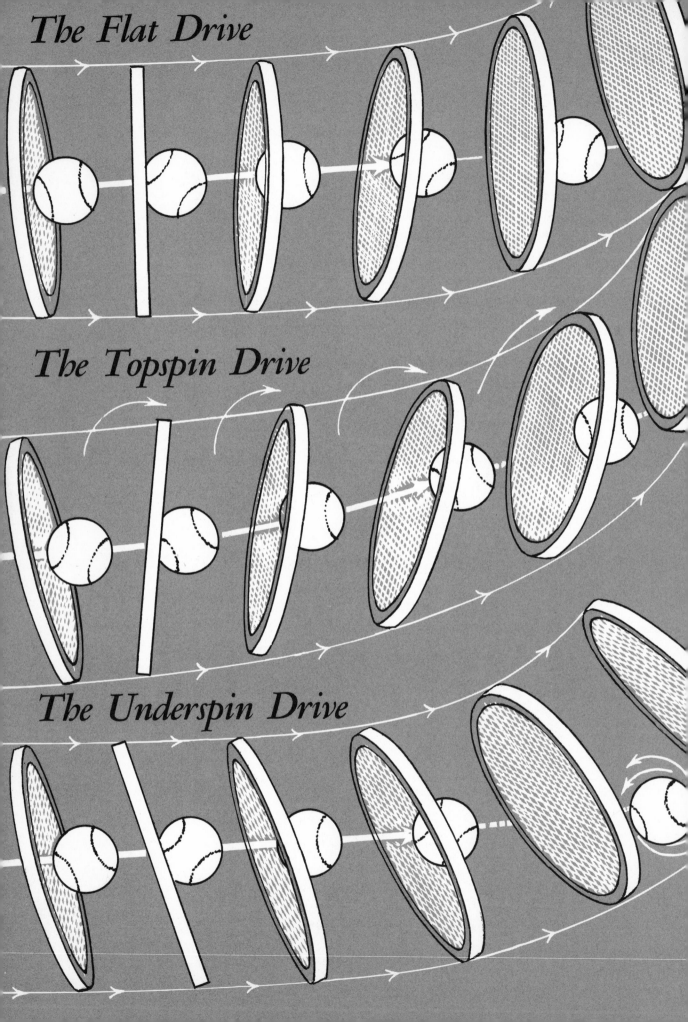

The Flat Drive

The Topspin Drive

The Underspin Drive

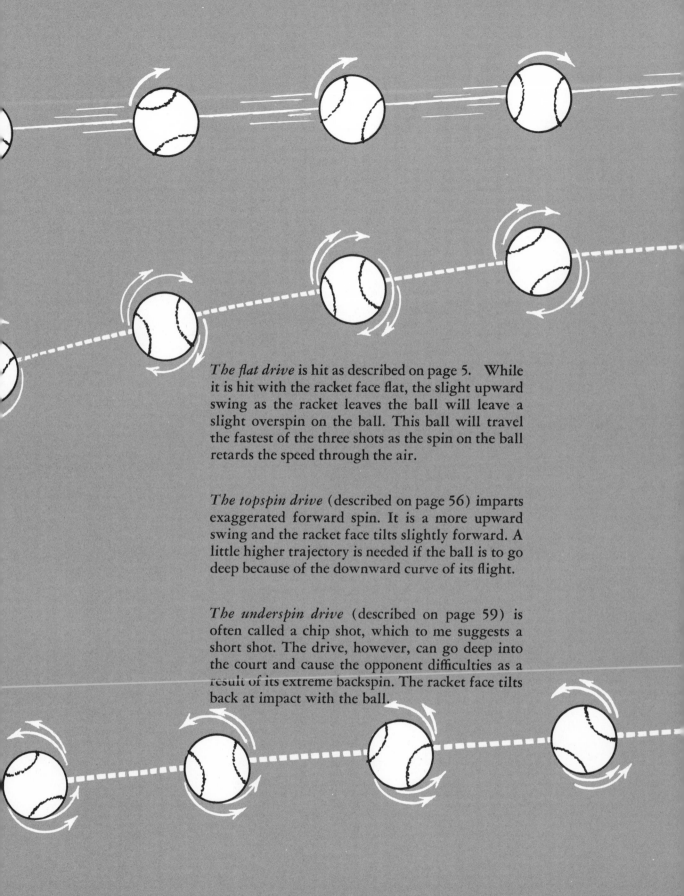

The flat drive is hit as described on page 5. While it is hit with the racket face flat, the slight upward swing as the racket leaves the ball will leave a slight overspin on the ball. This ball will travel the fastest of the three shots as the spin on the ball retards the speed through the air.

The topspin drive (described on page 56) imparts exaggerated forward spin. It is a more upward swing and the racket face tilts slightly forward. A little higher trajectory is needed if the ball is to go deep because of the downward curve of its flight.

The underspin drive (described on page 59) is often called a chip shot, which to me suggests a short shot. The drive, however, can go deep into the court and cause the opponent difficulties as a result of its extreme backspin. The racket face tilts back at impact with the ball.

The Topspin Drive

Bill Tilden said, "Mastery and complete knowledge of spin is of paramount importance to the good tennis player." Spin is important in two principal ways. It helps control the ball, and it fools the opponent, often forcing an error. The topspin is probably the most useful spin shot, and here are two typical uses for it. When you are deep in your own court and the ball bounces low, it allows you to hit hard and still keep it in the court. It curves down in flight, so it is essential for angled passing shots, particularly the short angles.

In making the backswing for the topspin drive, the body movements, balance, and so forth will be just about the same as those described for the flat forehand drive (page 4). The difference is that as the racket is swung back the face is opened more and the arc will be deeper. The forward course of the racket will be more upward and rotating over the ball as it is hit, imparting the topspin. More wrist is used than in the flat drive, but the same follow-through is necessary. The ball will have to be aimed higher to allow for its downward curve.

The Underspin Forehand Drive

This shot used to be called a chop shot (a misnomer) and seems to have come into great disrepute. And yet this is the same shot that is used by many of our top players on their backhand and called a chip shot, as I have already mentioned. It is a very useful shot at times, but as I have emphasized should not be used regularly, as no shot should be. It is a good defensive shot when you are hurried. It is not to be confused with some other *touch* spin shots or soft shots. It is followed through, with the racket face tilted slightly back, and should land deep in the opponent's court like any other drive.

The Backhand Topspin Drive

Note the shorter steps taken as the ball is reached. It is certainly easier to hit a good shot from an erect stance than when stretched out. In all essentials the backhand topspin drive is hit in the same manner as the forehand topspin drive. The swing should be started from about opposite the left shoulder and followed through, as described on page 10. This shot is possibly even more important in doubles than in singles, but in either case it is certainly true that a ball that is dipping down is harder to volley than a straight flat ball, no matter how fast it is traveling.

The Slice Shot—or Floater

This shot is used for the element of surprise. When after an exchange of hard back-court drives your opponent has made a rather short return, he may well expect you to hit hard to a corner and follow in to the net. This is logical, but just because of that, to change the tempo of the exchange, this shot could give you the advantage. With almost the same swing you can slow up the arm and slice across the ball under and from right to left, and aim for the deep center of the court. This gives the ball right-to-left and underspin. Because of the spin, the ball travels slowly through the air, and the extra time gives you a chance to get into the net at center. Your opponent has to hit a ball that is slow and spinning and changes his timing completely—his only chance is a very difficult short cross-court shot or lob.

The player who can use this shot, and build up a fairly certain easy win on the next return, is better equipped than the impetuous one who is over-eager for the kill.

The Effects of Spin

This page shows the effects of spin on the flight of the ball and on the bounce as related to the flat drive. The flat drive travels faster and therefore on a straighter line through the air until pulled down by gravity, and the bounce is medium. The deep topspin drive must be aimed higher because of its accentuated drop, and it will bounce high. This drop on the topspin shot will help keep the ball in court on sharply angled drives hit closer to the top of the net. The underspin drive has a tendency to rise slightly before starting to drop, and has a low, skidding bounce.

Of course the bounce of the ball, regardless of the type of shot, will vary on different types of court surfaces. This fact is, or should be, an in-

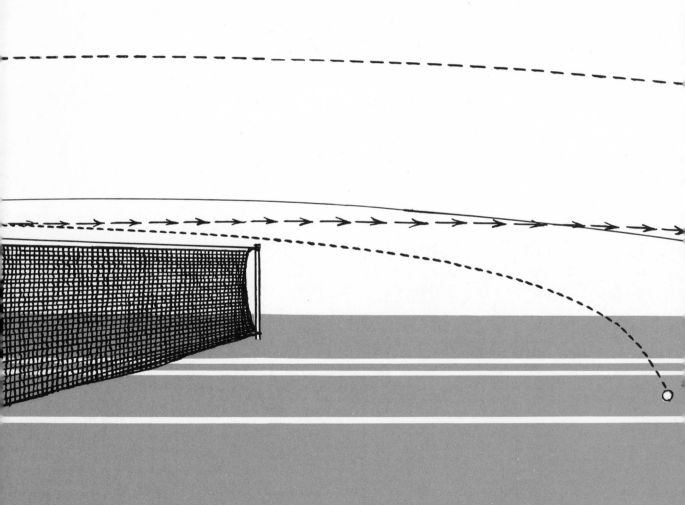

fluence on the kind of shots you use, particularly in a tournament match. There are many different surfaces, particularly now, when many new fabricated courts are being produced. So, to simplify, it is best to speak of them in two categories—that is, slow or fast courts; and although this might be construed to mean soft or hard courts, it does not necessarily follow.

Generally speaking, spin is more effective on rough surfaces than on smooth, particularly on the bounce. However, while spin takes hold less on a smooth surface, thus affecting the bounce less, it remains on the ball and has more effect on the opponent's shot.

The Topspin Drive
The Flat Drive
The Underspin Drive
The Short Topspin Drive

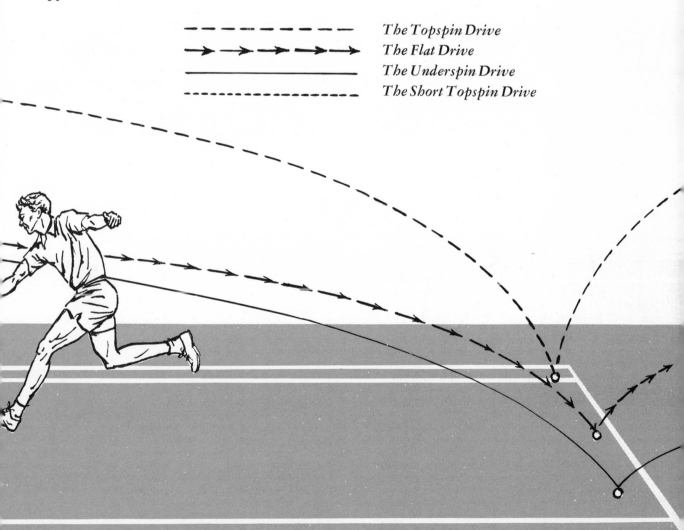

The Return of Spin Shots

Regardless of your own choice of shots to make during a match, your opponent is going to have the chance to make his choice of shots. They may be similar to yours, and in that case all you have to do is to be better at them than he is. But if he chooses to use what almost might be considered a different language which you don't understand and for which you have no answers, you are sunk. You must understand spin shots whether you choose to use them yourself or not. They are very apt to throw off your timing or even the direction of your shot, unless you recognize them by knowledge and observation as they are made, and are ready to meet them with your own answers.

At this point I must repeat my opinion that even you base your game on speed and power, you uld learn the spin and soft shots as adjuncts to r game for at least occasional use. It should not necessary for you to play tennis at one tempo— t is, play in a groove of timing. Sooner or later will meet an opponent who through knowl- e and variety of shots will break up your me. You must know all the answers. Your eye uld tell you when the other player hits with and what kind of spin it is, and you should w how you are going to hit it. To meet under- with a flat drive aim a little higher, as the spin l pull your shot down, and remember that the

opposite is true of topspin: it will raise your shot, possibly just enough to go out unless you allow for it. It is often a good idea to meet spin with spin, as this tends to take the spin off of the ball and give you more control. A good rule to remember is to return topspin with underspin and underspin with topspin. At right is the finish of the great Jack Kramer's high forehand shot.

The Forehand Drop Shot

The drop shot requires touch and should be used only when going in for a short ball. Obviously on this type of ball you have two choices—one is to hit deep and take the net, the other to outguess your opponent and dump it short. Of course a slow court favors this shot. It is made the same as the drop volley already described, except that as the ball has bounced it hangs in the air a little longer, and more slice, or underspin, may be applied.

The Backhand Drop Shot

The same things apply to this shot as have already been said about the forehand drop shot: the short backswing, and the delicacy of touch as the racket slices under the ball. An important part of this shot is deception. If you can take a big swing to suggest a drive and then stop your racket for the delicate shot, it gives you a big advantage. Obviously if he sees from your movements that you are going to make a drop shot it gives him a big jump.

The All-court Game

It seems to be the general idea that methods in anything improve with time—that old ways are naturally outmoded. The youngsters are particularly prone to this idea.

I believe that this is not true of tennis and that careful review of the description of the type of game Bill Tilden called the "all-court game" would be rewarding. Without repeating it (you can read it in his book) I will give the gist of it and why he felt it necessary to emphasize it thirty years ago. He deplored the fact that American players were ignoring the fundamentals of a basically sound, all-around game, sacrificing them for attack and power. This constant attacking game

has obvious faults. It wins or does not. There is alternative of a strong defense to give the pla time to recuperate physically and to plan a n type of attack. There is no thought given to stroying the opponent's game by having the swers to his shots and by changes of speed a placement to throw him off his game entirely then attack.

This emphasis on power that Tilden lamen thirty years ago has been going steadily in t direction. The timing of that type of game is v fine and the margin of safety very small. With necessity for our players to play all over the wo on different surfaces and in different weather

climates, a very sound defensive game seems indicated, from which to launch an attack built up by sound tactics. Our players are often heard to say they were tired, over-tennised, in a tournament. Surely a sound defensive game takes less out of a player, allows him to coast and feel out the opponent's game.

The player who best epitomized the all-court game since Tilden's time is Pancho Gonzales, and at his peak he was the world's best. He attacked. more consistently than Tilden but knew control of pace and could defend magnificently.

Practice

With good instruction anyone with an average mind and body can learn to play tennis—probably within one year. A willingness to apply oneself in the beginning to the basic principles of sound tennis will pay off later. There is no such thing as a natural-born tennis player. There are only people who have more than average physical ability and sense of timing, and the amount of desire one has to be a good player plus how much one is willing to practice is probably an accurate gauge of how good one will be.

Think of it in this way. If somebody said to you, "Do you play the piano?" and if you are able to barely pick out "Way Down upon the Swanee River" would you answer, "Oh, yes, I play the piano"? I think this is a fair analogy, and that most people who take up the game are satisfied with too little, much less than they are capable of even if they don't want to be a champion. As with most things, the better you do it, the more you enjoy it. From my observation the big stumbling block to improvement is the anxiety of most people to find someone they can beat. Mind you, I'm speaking of very poor or at least immature players. How they make the shots or whether they are improving doesn't matter. Of course they do not want to play with someone they can beat badly; they want a battle.

It is far from my intention to discourage anyone from playing the game. On the contrary, it has great rewards. I also do not suggest that anyone necessarily go through the long hours of rigorous training and practice necessary to being a top player.

But to be able to play the game pleasurably with good average players, I suggest the following routine:

1. Take some lessons.

2. Practice the two basic strokes, the forehand and backhand drive, until you can make them effortlessly, as easy as pointing your arm.

3. Learn to put the ball in play with your serve. The easiest way possible is to toss it up where it is easiest to hit, with a smooth backswing and coming forward rhythmically with the feeling you can put it where you want. Power, spin and so forth can be added later.

4. Think only of making the shot correctly when you start exchanging shots with another player, and have a general spot picked where you wish to put it. You can tell whether the shot is made well by the feel; don't worry whether it misses the line or not if it is well made. Accuracy will come later with more control.

5. Practice against a back wall to give yourself more balls to hit, more accuracy of return, and judgment of your stance in getting set for the bounce of the ball.

6. For at least two years try to get more satisfaction from hitting the ball well than in winning.

Playing the Angles

There seems to be an idea held by many tennis players (and not only beginners) that the idea of the game is "to put the ball where they ain't." In general this is true. But you should understand the possibilities of forcing an opponent into positions where he has the most difficult angles of return. This gives you the advantage.

There is a so-called center theory, illustrated here. Obviously a shot to the deep center of the opponent's court, followed to the net, forces him into short angled shots, but no straight-down-the-line shot. At the risk of repetitiousness, I must mention the old reliable, the lob, as a return from this spot.

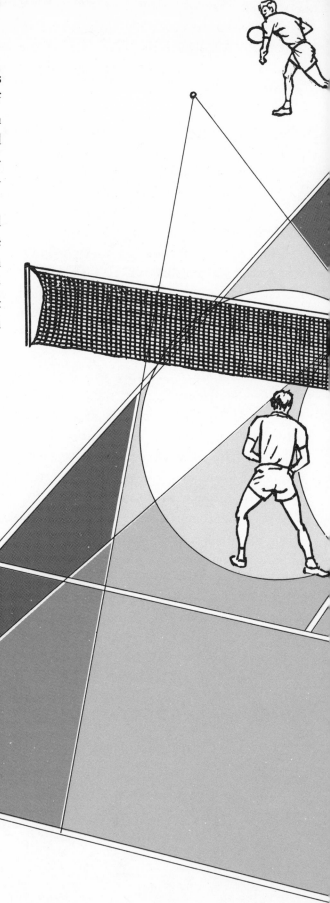

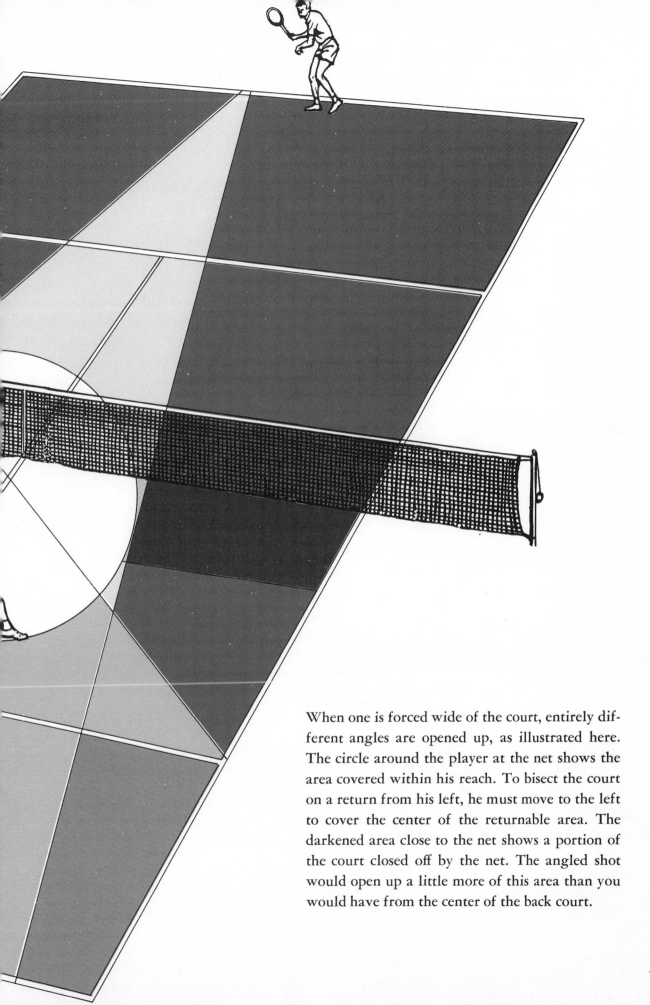

When one is forced wide of the court, entirely different angles are opened up, as illustrated here. The circle around the player at the net shows the area covered within his reach. To bisect the court on a return from his left, he must move to the left to cover the center of the returnable area. The darkened area close to the net shows a portion of the court closed off by the net. The angled shot would open up a little more of this area than you would have from the center of the back court.

Singles Tactics and Tournament Play

Unfortunately, too many players go into a match today with the idea that they are going to blast the opponent off the court. Knowledge of the "all-court game" is necessary to prepare yourself to defend as well as to attack.

Remember that most matches are lost, not won. That is to say that in most cases when you lose a match it is because you made more errors than the other player. There are very, very few cases where the analysis of a winning player's strokes in a match shows that he made more earned points than errors.

This by no means advocates playing a purely defensive game; it simply means giving one's opponent a chance to make errors.

Do not go on the court with a set plan of play, unless you know your opponent's game very well. Use the warm-up rallying period to study your opponent's strokes, as well as to get the feel of ball and the court yourself. You will notice s strengths and weaknesses in your opponent dur this period, but it would be wise to start play v an all-around steady game, with variety change of pace for a while to decide on your p of attack. This will give you a chance to see if is prone to errors and on what kind of shots.

In the meantime, it is possible your oppon has launched an attack against you, and an tack, of course, means taking the net.

Here is where your defense is put to the test, if it is good enough and his best shots are be returned, it is liable to force him into errors— also to discourage him. The fact that he quickly launched a net attack could very v mean that his ground strokes are weak.

n returning volleys, remember that by far your gest opening is in the air. Unless you can reach ball in good balance and see an opening, by all ans lob.

f your opponent is winning against your de- se, you must launch an attack. He may have a ak defense and the fact that you have waited for ur attack may surprise and upset him. A very d rule to remember is: "Always change a los- game, never change a winning one."

Psychology enters into the game to a large ex- t and in many ways this question is too compli- ed to go into here. However, you may run into kind of player who will try to intimidate you, ticularly if he has some reputation. Don't let n. You will also run into the kind of player who ll try to upset you with stalling tactics. Don't

let him. When you make an error, forget it, and when you are behind, concentrate all the more on winning.

I cannot overemphasize the use of variety, particularly in the early stages of a match. It will give you a chance to decide which strokes your opponent handles well and which poorly.

Exploit all parts of the court, not only from side to side but front to back, with variations of speed and spin. Do not let your opponent get into a set rhythm. If he loves a hard-driving exchange, break it up with soft spin shots. Never give him the shot he likes, even if it happens to be your best shot.

Your shots should all be hit with a definite spot and purpose in mind, whether it is to defend, maneuver or attack.

While this book deals mostly with tennis strokes, I should at least mention physical condition. Fine condition is absolutely essential as part of a fine player's equipment. Leaps and stretches are con-stantly required, and balance must be kep[t] [in] order to hit the ball effectively. This activity, [com]-pared to the ballet, is even more strenuous[, as] there is no prearranged choreography.

The Game of Doubles

Although the same shots are used in doubles as in singles, the volley and serve become even more important and the ground strokes are used less. The return of service, however, is vitally important in doubles and more difficult, because you have the net man opposite you to shut off part of the court.

The tactics in doubles are quite different from singles, and it is most important for good doubles play that both members of a team realize this and play accordingly. Outside of ability in the use of the various strokes, and a knowledge of the doubles game and its tactics, I believe it is necessary for a player to *like* doubles in order to be a very good doubles player.

It is well known that many of the fine singles players of the past have not been good at doub and there are others not so famous at singles w are famous as doubles players. I believe that difference lies in especially liking doubles pl For instance, it is safe to say that a player with gr serve and fine volley, even with only medic ground strokes, probably would make a be doubles player than another player with gr ground strokes and ordinary volley and serve.

In pointing out the big differences between two games, my purpose is to try to interest m people in the doubles game. The first step surel to help them understand it.

With the rapid increase in the number of peo taking up tennis today, there is a consequent l

ourts to accommodate them. Almost all clubs
overcrowded, and this can't help but result in
necessity to double up.

'm sure there are many people playing tennis
exercise. That is, they have lots of energy, and
love to chase that ball, and when they reach it,
ck it—the harder the better. This is not ten-
In tennis the pleasure for the average player
uld be not only in the exercise but in the ability
it the ball smoothly and with control. In other
rds, the pleasure of craftsmanship. Winning
uld be secondary until you really hit the ball
l.

t is quite an unpleasant sight to see, as one does
quently, four individuals who through lack of

space have been forced to play on the same court
and instead of playing doubles, each is trying to
play singles.

On the other hand, what is more pleasant than
to see four players playing a knowledgeable game
of doubles, each cognizant of his part. Teamwork
is the essence of good doubles play.

Here is a fine example of a doubles team which has fallen into one of the most common and basic errors of doubles tactics. The players have lined up the wrong way, in tandem fashion, leaving both sides wide open. The other team has not only stayed parallel but has taken the net. When serving, join your partner at the net as soon as possible.

85

Return of Service

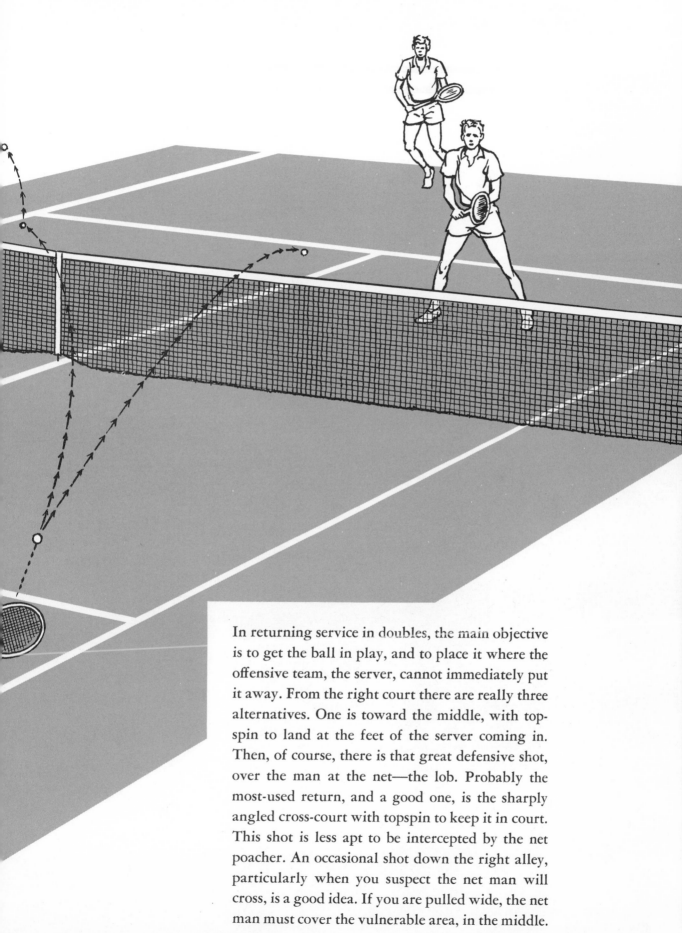

In returning service in doubles, the main objective is to get the ball in play, and to place it where the offensive team, the server, cannot immediately put it away. From the right court there are really three alternatives. One is toward the middle, with topspin to land at the feet of the server coming in. Then, of course, there is that great defensive shot, over the man at the net—the lob. Probably the most-used return, and a good one, is the sharply angled cross-court with topspin to keep it in court. This shot is less apt to be intercepted by the net poacher. An occasional shot down the right alley, particularly when you suspect the net man will cross, is a good idea. If you are pulled wide, the net man must cover the vulnerable area, in the middle.

Opening the Court

I have mentioned the center theory in singles, and it is even more important in doubles. The return angle shots are more difficult from the center. Also, a ball in the center is bound to cause a question as to which partner should take it. Thus a build-up shot should be made first, a sharply

angled shot, either fast with topspin or soft with underspin, to pull one partner wide, leaving the middle open.

The correct answer to this situation is for the partner of the man pulled wide to move toward the middle to letter A. Anticipation is a word often mentioned in tennis; it is not a gift; it comes from experience—the experience of learning a probable return from a specific position.

Poaching

When you are at the net and your partner is serving, watch the pattern of the opponents' returns. If
you decide that the returns are not very sharply
angled across-court, you may decide to cross over
and intercept it with a volley. Two things are involved in taking this chance: one is that you should
let your partner know of your intention, either by
a prearranged signal or by telling him; the other is
that you must make your volley a winner. If it is
not, the chances are that you have left your team in
a vulnerable position. If your opponent has guessed
your intention and puts it down your alley, you are
out of luck if it goes in.

Returning the Twist Serve

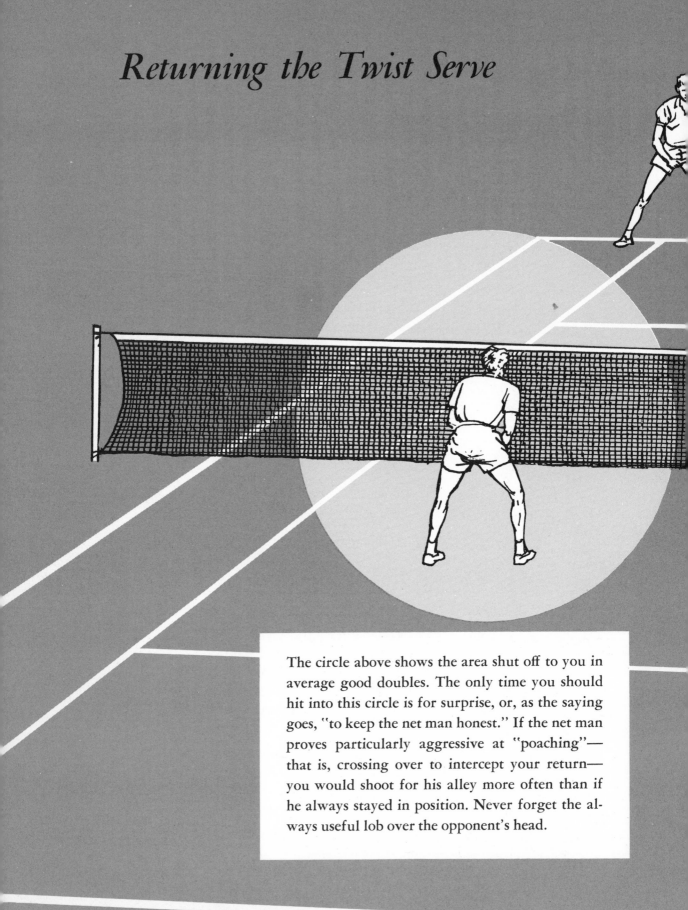

The circle above shows the area shut off to you in average good doubles. The only time you should hit into this circle is for surprise, or, as the saying goes, "to keep the net man honest." If the net man proves particularly aggressive at "poaching"—that is, crossing over to intercept your return—you would shoot for his alley more often than if he always stayed in position. Never forget the always useful lob over the opponent's head.

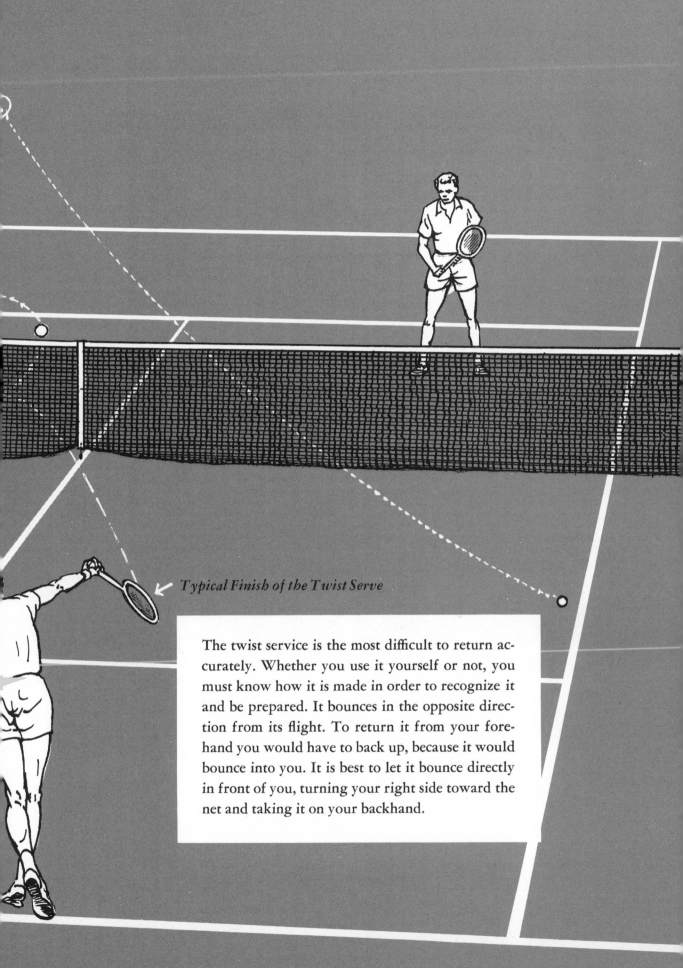

Typical Finish of the Twist Serve

The twist service is the most difficult to return accurately. Whether you use it yourself or not, you must know how it is made in order to recognize it and be prepared. It bounces in the opposite direction from its flight. To return it from your forehand you would have to back up, because it would bounce into you. It is best to let it bounce directly in front of you, turning your right side toward the net and taking it on your backhand.

The Lob Volley

In good modern doubles, with the emphasis on both sides being to command the net, it often happens that all four players are inside of the service line exchanging volleys. This is apt to end with what golfers call sudden death—one player putting up a sitter which one of the opponents kills. In this situation, a shot which can end the point suddenly is the lob volley, and it depends on touch and thinking. It is really a very sensible shot but a difficult one, because it is a sudden change of timing. But the back court is the open spot, and the beauty of the shot is that it is unexpected—and has to be, or it could be intercepted. Surprise cannot be overemphasized in tennis. (Arthur Ashe here shown making the shot.)

Yours? — This ridiculous situation can happen even with very good players. It is absolutely necessary for a give-and-take attitude to exist on a doubles team. There must be confidence in each other and the feeling that the other man is always doing his best for the team. However, each player must be constantly aware of the other's place on the court. You should always "call" a shot when there is a question.

would seem here that in the rapid exchange at
net the player about to hit the ball is in the cat-
seat. If with the same swing he can make a fast
volley, it should be a winner. The pair on this
seem to be closing in to protect the center, so a
p angled volley to the right player's alley
ld probably win the point.

Women's Tennis

Until the 1920s it was not considered ladylike or even womanly for the female of the species to participate in sports. It is true that lawn tennis parties were held, and amidst much giggling the ladies would take the court holding their voluminous skirts up with one hand and with the other pat the ball at the net in something resembling battledore and shuttlecock.

In the 1920s there was a renaissance, and Molla Mallory began a women's tennis game that within its physical limitations began to approximate the men's. Skirts were shortened and women really began to run and hit the ball. Mrs. Mallory was closely followed by other greats—Helen Wills, Suzanne Lenglen and Helen Jacobs. It was still almost entirely a back-court game depending on steadiness and court covering.

Gradually, the ladies began to try to emulate the men and did go in to the net occasionally. Helen Jacobs started this trend, and I played with her once in a while at Forest Hills.

Since the 1920s, women's tennis has advanced as much, if not more, than men's. It is more difficult for women to reach the net, but when they do, many of them volley very well. In a back-court exchange of drives of equal pace and speed, a top-ranking woman player would probably outsteady a man of equal rank.

To sum up, the difference in the two games is based on physical differences. Unquestionably, men hit harder and cover court much faster than women do.

Mixed Doubles

All the general tactics pertaining to men's doubles should apply to mixed doubles. The only difference is that in mixed doubles it is assumed that the woman is weaker. Based on this assumption (which is not always true), the woman should defend as much of the court as she can and let the man be the aggressor. The things for the average woman to keep in mind are that when she finds herself placed at the net, she stays there and tries to return anything she can reach. The only shot the lady has to hit is the *serve* to her. If she is having difficulty with that, she should by all means lob. The woman should not try to take the net on her serve, but if possible come in on her first return.

Court Surfaces

Most games have standardized conditions of play. The tennis ball has been pretty much standardized, but court surfaces vary more today than ever before, and new ones are being introduced continually. The game is difficult enough to master without having to adapt to many different kinds of bounces and variations of speed.

Strangely enough, our national championship is played on the surface that the fewest number of players ever have a chance to play on—grass. The few grass courts in existence are gradually disappearing because of the difficulty and expense of keeping them up. Add to that the fact that they are fragile and wear badly. Also, by the final rounds of

a championship a close match may be decided by a bad bounce. It seems certain that grass courts are doomed, and before many years another surface will replace them. This is unfortunate, because at its best grass is the finest surface to play on.

A new development in the game is the rapid increase in the new indoor facilities for winter play. The court surfaces vary from very little to a great deal, and so does the lighting—another condition to cope with. The new compositions in manufactured court surfaces today are too many to mention. They vary in color (different shades of red, green or gray), as well as in speed and sureness of footing.

Coping with Courts

What has been said about strokes, equipment and court tactics are generalizations which should apply to the average court. The fact is that the average player plays his game the same on any court —with one thought, to get the ball back in the other court.

If you have achieved a fair amount of regularity of return among players of your class, it may disturb your timing to play on a strange surface, and throw your stroke off.

There are so many variations in the speed and kind of bounce on different surfaces that it is impossible to cover them all, so here are a few generalizations.

1. A smooth hard surface leaves the speed on the ball, leaves the spin on the ball, which will bounce low from a hard hit.

2. A coarse soft surface will slow up the speed, take spin off the ball (affecting the bounce), which will generally bounce higher and slower.

These are the two extremes, and the variations in between you will have to judge for yourself.

The power game, big serve, net rushing, and the hard volley are overwhelmingly favored by the hard fast court.

On the other hand, the all-court player, equipped with a variety of shots, guile, physical agility and stamina, will probably toy with the power player on a soft court.

My conclusions are that the all-court player will beat the power player in the long run on a majority of courts; this is, of course, assuming the all-court player also has a good attacking game.

Weather Conditions

I have already mentioned that it is not always enough to learn a rhythmic, grooved swing on courts you are accustomed to—and with players who return the ball in an accustomed way.

Different surfaces of court which affect the bounce of the ball in an unaccustomed way have also been mentioned. Another element you will encounter if you play tournaments is the weather. Wind and rain, either together or alone, can create havoc with your shots and, of course, under these conditions the importance of soundness and adaptability are stressed. A finely tuned game may go to pieces.

Here are a few general principles to remember in *wind*.

1. Greater concentration than ordinarily is needed.

2. Hit flat—in general, use less spin with the wind.

3. Against the wind, underspin shots are best.

4. Take the net as much as possible when playing with the wind.

5. Use the lob a good deal against the wind. On damp or wet courts the net game should be used less because of insecure footing. Control and mixed spin are of great value.

6. Outguessing the opponent is of particular importance because of the difficulty of changing direction on slippery courts.

For the Beginner

DO

Take some lessons to establish correct form.

Watch the ball when you contact it.

Watch the ball when your opponent contacts it.

Always aim the ball at a definite spot.

Turn hips and body sideways to the net so as
to swing through the ball.

Try to contact the ball in front of you.

Keep the weight (body) moving into the contact
of the ball.

Keep the racket in ready position after each shot.

Toss the ball up slowly when serving.

Bend the knees, for low balls.

DON'T

Use much wrist until control is achieved.

Face the net when contacting the ball.

Drop the racket head below the wrist.

Loosen the grip of the racket on contact.

Try to hit hard before getting control and feel.

Step on the line or inside the court on the serve
until after contact with the ball.

Use spins or slices or trick shots until your
stroke is solid.

Rush your shots.

Shorten the swing for the second serve.

Try to win at the sacrifice of good execution.